CHRISTIAN'S MANY ADVENTURES ON HIS WALK TO PRIMARY SCHOOL

BY RAINA PARKER

INSPIRED BY CHRISTIAN PARKER

Donated to Henley Library
with every good wish
from
Raina & Christian

June 2024

DISCLAIMER

This is a work of factual nonfiction and is written for entertainment purposes only. The writings are solely observations from a child and were recorded by me with no malice, unkindness, harm or hurt intended. Any persons who might recognize themselves are thanked for brightening my son's day.

****

This memoir was inspired by my son, Christian. It is a collection of Christian's thoughts and observations during his daily walk to primary school, St Paul's School, Wooburn Green, and recorded by me, his Mum.

My intention for putting my son's observations on paper (besides a Christmas present for him), was to record and document details of how a child on the autistic spectrum sees the world.

Christian's sisters never commented on what they saw on their walks to school, so I soon began to realise that Christian's attention to detail was unique, due to his ADHD and autistic brain. He helped me see the world through his eyes just by listening to what he was describing in front of him.

In Christian's early years of his school life, he did feel very different because of the way he saw things. His peers also treated him differently for it and would make fun of him. This made Christian feel very isolated and at times very lonely. I hope by sharing his observations through this memoir, that other neuro-divergent children reading this will feel a connection with Christian and they won't feel as lonely as he did.

THE PEOPLE WE MET

Before Covid:

These are observations Christian made before Covid:

The Greyhound Couple

When Christian first started at St Paul's School we would often 'park and stride' meaning we would drive halfway to school, park the car and then walk a short distance to the school entrance. This worked well as Christian would be in a push chair, and his 2 sisters would be walking alongside us. Christian's younger sister out of the 2, was only at Nursery so a careful eye was needed on her especially as Cores End Road is very narrow in places.

Most mornings we used to see a couple walking their dog along the grass bank by Slate Meadow. They owned an old grey-coloured greyhound who walked very slowly. They were a friendly couple who would often wave or shout 'hello' to us if they were a distance away. As time went by the dog walked slower and slower. Sadly, the dog died about four years ago; the year before Christian went into Year 5. After that we would often see the male owner walking by himself. He had a certain unmistakeable gait and was tall and very slim. To Christian he looked like his old greyhound dog as his physique was the same as his dog - lean and thin. The gentleman walked the same route he once did with his greyhound.

On one particular morning, we saw both the man and woman together, enjoying a walk past the school entrance as we too were approaching it. We automatically waved and shouted out 'hello' as they passed on the opposite side of the street but sadly, they didn't appear to recognise us and didn't acknowledge us. This made Christian feel very sad.

'Motor Man' George

We often saw a friend's husband, George, on his way to work. He rode a black moped at the time and often wore a black coat, black Jeans, and a black helmet with a tiny camera attached to the top of it. The moped was his pride and joy. George would always wave – and sometimes pressed his tooting horn as he drove past. This man would often do a little finger wave, releasing his index finger from his handlebars. It was a little finger wave, rather than a big wave with one hand. Somehow our friend's husband managed to keep his hands on the handlebar at all times, which impressed Christian greatly. Christian thought that took a lot of skill to do.

The 'Speedy Scooter Guy'

We started to see a young man, in his early 20s, shoot out of Willows Drive each morning on an electric scooter. Thank goodness no-one was walking past on the footpath at the same time as there would have been a nasty collision due to the speed he was going! We think he was a young trainee teacher heading to the local Secondary School. He would whizz along at a fair lick, dodging any bumps on the pavement on the way. (The pavement is a narrow one and dangerous due to the flow of traffic whipping by without adding a speeding scooter to the mix!) This young man was agile, had great balance and skill in controlling his scooter. He used to bounce and glide along seamlessly. Christian was in awe of his agility. Thankfully we were often on the other side of the road when we spotted him. This man had skill in controlling his balance.

The 'happy grey-haired postman'

This postman has been delivering post in our local area for well over 20 years. All the time we walked to school (except during the pandemic), we would see this very cheerful postman who always smiled and waved at us. He would often utter 'Good morning' as we walked on by or passed each other on the pavement. He would be delivering letters to all the houses along Cores End Road. As he was always smiling, he seemed a very happy man to Christian so he called him the 'happy grey-haired postman' to distinguish him amongst the other postmen in the village. He wore a postman's uniform and he had very grey hair with a warm and friendly smile.

The 'Bin Sweeper!'

This was the name Christian gave to a road sweeper. We used to see a man sat inside a small vehicle, (we can only describe as a tuk-tuk style) road sweeper. It was so small that it was only large enough for one slim man to sit inside it. The Road Sweeper would mount the pavement to clean them in both Bourne End and Wooburn Green. (We have seen him at Marlow too! ‘He’s followed us!’ exclaimed Christian one day).

We would often meet ‘the bin sweeper’ along Slate Meadow on the Brookbank pavement. This is a wide pavement. It was always a joy to see him. Christian remarked that the man came from India because of the style of vehicle he was sat in! It did genuinely look like a converted tuk-tuk! Christian believed that he had been sweeping all around the world 'cleaning the pavements!' To Christian it made perfect sense. This was the reason, Christian explained to me, is why we would only see him once every 3-4 months.

On one occasion, after passing the 'bin Sweeper man', Christian said, 'If he went to Mars, how long would it take?' I was rather puzzled and said it would take years for him to get there. Christian went on 'Just imagine if he could portal up to Mars? How clean Mars would be if he went there!' I marvelled at Christian's great imagination.

We had not seen 'the Bin Sweeper man' for some time and one morning Christian commented that it was about time he came back to our area. And then he magically appeared in May 2021. Christian would always look out for 'the bin sweeper man' because this gentleman would always wave and wait for us to walk past him before he continued to clean the pavements. Without him cleaning the pavements they became thick with mud, causing them to be very slippery and mucky, especially after a lot of rainfall. Christian is so glad and grateful for this man’s role in society. He provides a much-needed service.

‘The Childminder Gang’

Most mornings we met a group of children with a childminder walking towards us. (I had seen this particular childminder for over 17 years walking different children to school). This was the name Christian gave them because there were several children with the childminder and they looked like a gang to him. The children were friendly and would always say hello to

Christian. They were heading towards school too, but not St Paul's School. There were usually six children walking and at least 2 of them knew Christian from Cubs and Scouts.

However, after lockdown seeing them became quite stressful for Christian, as on more than one occasion we had to walk onto the road in order to adhere to the 2 metre rule. The joy of seeing them became a worry for him.

The Bakery sisters

Every morning we always walked past our village bakery on The Parade as this was on our daily route to school. No matter who they were serving, if we were seen by the 2 ladies or their manager, they would always stop what they were doing, smile, and would give Christian the biggest of waves if we happen to catch their eye. (This bakery is somewhere we like to go for a rare treat – Christian loves their bacon rolls, and I love their cookies!) They have known my family for years so they would always wave at us, no matter what time of day it was. When we came out of the first lockdown, our school hours altered, and Christian was really worried that we might not see them again. He needn't have worried, because they were still there, and they continued to wave. Because of their kindness towards him, Christian realised it was special to be local and to be known by the shop keepers.

'Bourne for Desserts' man

We would see this kind gentleman setting up his café every morning. He would often be setting up his outdoor furniture and umbrellas as we walked by. (This was another favourite shop of ours as the ice creams and desserts were amazing. They used to do Knickerbocker glories and coke floats. Christian's favourite was the bubble gum ice cream, and he would enjoy this in an ice-cream cone with 2 scoops. He would always stop what he was doing, smile and say 'good morning' every time he saw us. Christian always puzzled over who might want ice-cream for breakfast – and he always hoped the man would open earlier so he could buy one! (Tragically though during 2022, not long after Christian had moved to Secondary School, this business closed and remains greatly missed by the locals).

Ted

For many of our years walking to St Pauls School, we would see Ted. He was a harmless old chap and was always in a wheelchair, because he had lost one of his legs. It turned out from chatting with him, that he had been a local man to Wooburn Green all his life. He used to whizz along on the pavement to the betting shop in

Bourne End, every day to place a bet, come rain or shine. We started to meet Ted when we would part walk to school (having left our car in Brookhouse drive to walk the final stretch to school along the path at Brookbank and Slate Meadow). Ted seemed a very lonely man and because I would say 'Good Morning' he started to slow down and stop for a chat. It turned out that I was right; he was very lonely. He meant well but he was, in Christian's words 'very odd'.

Ted started to wait to see us in the mornings. He was not the tidiest, cleanest or the happiest of folk, but we always lifted his spirits when he saw us, and it would make Ted smile. As time went on and I got to know Ted, I found out he had lived in Wooburn Green all his life, with his late wife in a flat (a group of flats at the bottom of Brook drive). Sadly, the block of flats where Ted lived were closed down, as the land had been sold to developers, and Ted was forced to move to Bourne End. Ted was really upset to have to make this move to Bourne End. He was very proud to live in Wooburn Green all his life, so he really didn't want to move out of the village to Bourne End. Sadly, Ted passed away not long after he had been relocated to Bourne End. Christian liked Ted and missed seeing him in the mornings. He was quite a character.

The 'Hearing Dog' Man

Some mornings, if we were running a little late, we would drive to a road close to St Paul's School and park our car to walk the rest of the journey to school. A mum who had a son in my daughter's class lived in the same road and encouraged me to park outside her house. Often when we did this, we would meet a man walking a puppy. He would always have a springer spaniel puppy that was really lively, very excited and friendly. The puppy would often jump up which Christian really didn't like. 'They are not supposed to do this!' Christian would remark. He often wore shorts so he would feel the puppy's claws on his legs, which hurt him. Christian became nervous of the puppy as a result. The man was very friendly and told us he looked after puppies for the Hearing dogs charity for the first six months of their lives, and then they would go back to the Hearing Dog charity for training. On a few occasions the gentleman had been lucky enough to meet our late Queen because of the work he did for the charity. Over time we met quite a few of the puppies this man looked after, who all were given names from the Star Wars films. We had great admiration for this gentleman. Some mornings we would see him driving off in his car to take the puppy for a walk to the woods or park. The gentleman would bring the puppy over to see us as part of familiarising the puppy with different people of different ages. It was a joy to meet them even though Christian didn't like them very much. He preferred to see them from inside the man's car in the mornings than walking over to greet him!

The Dog Whisperer

Most mornings on our walk to school Christian and I would see a very tall, thin man walk past our house or sometimes we would see him walking along the Parade with his dog. The man's dog was not on a lead and obeyed this man's vocal commands.

The dog was a beautiful border collie cross. The gentleman would stride along as the dog would jog by his side trying to keep up. Occasionally the man had two dogs with him. He very rarely spoke or smiled, but when he did, his face lit up. He always seemed to be acutely aware of everything going on about him yet looked deep in thought. To Christian this man seemed indifferent to people, minding his own business and very rarely engaged in any lengthy conversation with anyone we seemed to know. It is a shame that he only spoke if we greeted him first. Some mornings he would stride by so quickly that it was too late to say hello. Christian thought this man didn't like us as the gentleman showed a real reluctance to speak to us. (I later found out he is a retired policeman).

Christian's sister's best friend

On one walk to school in 2019, we met a new girl on her first day at St Paul's School. She was the same age as Christian's sister. This young girl became Christian's sister's best friend from that day forward. Not only did

Christian's sister greet her warmly but she was the first person to arrive in her year to school that day. Christian also liked this girl as she always spoke to him in the mornings on the playground. She would often come to our house during the school holidays for sleepovers. (Both girls are now at college together and although they are studying different subjects, they are still the best of friends).

The 'Bag Lady'

Christian noticed a friendly looking, short lady with a round face, when we first started walking to school. She wore spectacles and rocked side-to-side as she walked along. She was quite plump and a happy lady who would be walking towards Wooburn Green. Every morning she would greet us with a smile and a ‘hello’. In the winter months she would often wear a long coat and a scarf of the Queen around her shoulders. To Christian, she reminded him of being someone’s Nana because she was “round and happy”. We used to see this lady every day up until September 2020 but we stopped seeing her after that time. Christian thought she could have been a schoolteacher as she always carried a handbag and a reusable shopping bag. She looked to be in her late 50s. Her expression led us to think she was in pain until she saw us and then she smiled. She seemed to struggle carrying her bags too.

The Coffee Cup Couple

Since we started walking to school in the mornings we used to see, at least once a week, a man in his early 60s who wore a lightweight anorak and trainers. He also had a rucksack on his back. This man was tall and wore glasses, or sometimes sunglasses depending on the weather. Christian noticed he had a bald head and hair around the sides of his face (rather like sideburns).

This man would often walk past us on his way to Bourne End. Christian observed that he always clutched some form of a coffee cup! Sometimes it looked like a travelling one from home or a disposable cup from a coffee shop. We soon worked out he liked to walk to the local coffee shop in Bourne End.

After lockdown his wife accompanied him on his daily walk. Both of them would always smile and say hello.

The Hooded One!

Every morning we would see a man walking to Wooburn Green. He was in his mid-20s and always wore black clothing. He strode along with his hands in his pockets, always wearing a hoodie with the hood up (or an outer coat over the top of his hoodie). He would carry a black rucksack on his back and in the summer, he wore sunglasses. He would be walking in the same direction as us, often overtaking us which was ok until after lockdown. He refused to observe the 2-metre rule and he would march past us, often brushing one of us with his elbow. Due to wearing trainers we did not hear him coming and one of us would jump when he appeared beside us. He never spoke even though we saw him most mornings. Christian thought he was very rude because he would march past us and never spoke when he did pass. Christian noticed this man wore air pods in his ears so Christian concluded this was the reason why he never uttered a word to us.

The School Teacher

During 2019, for almost a year, we saw a very casually smartly dressed young man, in his early 20s, walking to the local Secondary school. Depending on the time, we would pass him at Slate Meadow, or along Cores End Road. He would smile and always stepped onto the grass verge to let us pass. He was very upright and straight when he walked and had black hair. Sometimes he wore a tracksuit and trainers but most of the time he wore smart trousers and a jumper. After lockdown we stopped seeing him, as our school time changed, which meant we were walking to school much earlier than this gentleman, so we no longer passed him. However, Christian still looked out for him every day as seeing him had become part of Christian's morning routine.

You Tuber Guy

Christian noticed a teenage lad, in casual attire, carrying a rucksack on his back, and of Korean descent. According to Christian, this teenager wore an earpiece and was aged around 18. We would meet him walking past Slate Meadow. He always walked very briskly and seemed to be in a rush. He was tall and slim. Christian thought he was a 'you tuber' guy on Minecraft that he was following on YouTube at the time, and he would tell me that every time we saw him. When I said to Christian that I doubted that very much, he promptly replied 'He is his double then'. Christian was really serious about it and was convinced he was right.

The Commuter Looking Teacher

Often, we would see an older gentleman, in his 50s, walking to the local Secondary school. For some time, we thought this gentleman was a commuter, heading into an office in London, because he often looked smart, wore a dark suit and tie, wearing either black or tanned leather polished shoes, as well as a long, faun coloured raincoat. This man carried a satchel type leather bag that could have contained a laptop and paperwork. He wore dark rimmed glasses and was balding slightly. This gentleman often smiled at us but he never spoke. Christian thought he looked like Mr Bumble from the West End musical 'Oliver' or that he would make a great Santa Claus too.

The Straight Lady

Quite often we used to see a very smart, upright lady who had very pointy facial features including a very pointed nose. She was slim, tall and middle-aged with straight, shoulder-length dark hair. This lady often carried a carrier bag and had a handbag over her shoulder. She often wore black trousers. When we first saw her this woman never smiled at us or said hello but, overtime, she mellowed and spoke ‘hello’ and smiled at us. To Christian she looked severe and unapproachable, but when she smiled, she seemed very nice.

A mother, 2 children and a cocker poodle

Most mornings, before lockdown, we would see this family with their puppy who was a cocker poodle. They would be walking towards the local schools, as her children wore the uniforms from both schools. We knew the family as they had their daughter at St. Paul's School until she left to go to Secondary school. The cocker poodle was very lively and so friendly. He liked to jump up at Christian especially, to say hello. Christian did not like this very much so would very quickly say 'hello' and hurry past. The dog always scratched him when it did jump up and this hurt Christian. I would often see the Mum on the way back for school drop off so we would stop for a quick chat. She was very kind as well as friendly to us both.

After lockdown sadly we never stopped to talk. That social element disappeared because of Covid. Gradually they stopped moving out of the way to let us past, so we always stepped into a hedge or onto the road between New Road and La Maison shop where we met them every school morning in order to let them pass safely.

Blonde-Haired Lady

Regularly in the mornings we would see a blonde-haired, tall, slim upright lady and her son walking to a local school on our way to school in the mornings. We started to see them when Christian's sister walked with us. As time went by, we sometimes would spot the lady jogging having dropped her son to the local primary school. Other times she would be jogging, and her son would be riding his bike to school beside her. (Occasionally I would see her on my return home riding her son's bike back home or jogging). Often, she wore a bright pink raincoat; other times she was smartly dressed for the office. She looked very elegant due to her posture, whether she was running or walking. Her hair was long and straight that went down to her waist. She would often thank us if we moved out of her path and would say 'good morning'.

The Itinerant Musician

We would often see a dishevelled looking gentleman, who looked to be in his late 50s, walking towards us. To Christian, he looked like the Eccentric

Scientist from the blockbuster movie, 'Back to the Future'! His hair was fair, unkempt, shoulder length and very wild looking! Other times Christian would say he looked like a musician.

He dressed like 'Elton John' and he had black round rimmed glasses. He wore either jeans or black trousers, donned with a tan-coloured casual jacket and trainers. Sometimes his shirt had become untucked. He looked laid back and relaxed as he walked at a very leisurely, staggering pace. Christian noticed he always carried a well-worn, shabby looking, soft brown leather bag over his shoulder which looked very much like a laptop bag. Christian thought he may be heading to Bourne End station to catch a train to Paddington. This gentleman never spoke to us but would always pass us and give us a nod of his head to say hello.

After lockdown we still saw him on the school run. He was wearing similar clothing, but he no longer carried his brown leather bag. Christian thought he must be heading to the local coffee shop! He was always very considerate, and he would pass us giving us plenty of room, by stepping off the pavement, or would cross to the other side of the road, in order to keep to the 2m social distance rule.

On one such occasion this man almost got clipped by a passing car! He was crossing the road, using the zebra crossing, as a car was turning into the Bourne End Business Park (next to the zebra crossing at the bottom of New Road). The car did not slow down or let the gentleman continue across the zebra crossing. Instead, the driver increased speed and swerved around him on the crossing! The gentleman raised his fist and swore at the driver. Christian was very shocked by the driver's attitude and couldn't believe the car almost hit this nice man.

The Rude Cyclist

Regularly we would meet three young teenagers cycling to the local Secondary school. We would often meet them along Brookbank, where there is a large grass area and weeping willow trees. Two of the cyclists would always cycle around us, giving us lots of space as they went past – but one refused to move. He would ride at us, forcing us to step or leap on the grass verge so he could remain on the tarmac path. This was a deliberate act done to intimidate us and scare Christian which he successfully achieved every time. It was not very nice, pleasant or kind. On one occasion this same lad almost caught Christian's arm which frightened him all the more. Since September 2021 we would only see one lad cycling by himself - and he always moved onto the grass.

The ‘Idiot Cyclist’

At least once a week we would spot another two young teenage lads cycling in the middle of the road along the A4155 at Cores End Roundabout or along The Parade. They did wheelies for a prank or laugh on their way to the local Secondary school (lifting the front part of their bicycle off the floor so they were balanced on one wheel whilst pedalling frantically to keep their bike up on its back wheel). As anyone local would know, this road is extremely busy at school run hour, so it was both reckless and dangerous to pull this stunt.

Occasionally the same lads cycled on the path, and they did a similar act, on the pavement as they passed you. They were undoubtedly foolish and definitely not cool. In the words of Christian they were, quite simply, 'Idiots'! He was very unimpressed by their stunts.

During Covid:

These are observations after the 1st lockdown which I have entitled during Covid:

Tank Top Man

On this particular morning, we almost walked into this man, which in itself was terrifying as we were advised by the Government to keep one's distance and not to be closer than 2 metres apart whether indoors or outdoors, (which was described as adhering to 'the 2-metre rule'). The man was wearing faded blue jeans with an old-fashioned silver metal key chain that was fastened to his belt and the keys were attached. The keys were safely out of sight and inside his pocket. The man had tattoos on his tanned arms; was bald and stocky and about the same height as Christian. We were busy chatting and due to a hedgerow, that had overgrown during lockdown, we were obscured from each other's line of vision. We did not see this man coming as the incident occurred on a bend at the top of Furlong Road. We hadn't been out of lockdown for long, so it was terrifying when we saw him striding at us. He refused to move out of the way, and he wasn't wearing a mask. The only way we were able to avoid him was to step into the overgrown hedgerow that was lining the path. The man was in such a hurry and didn't break stride once. He simply confidently and determinedly marched past us. This man was wearing a white vest, which is why Christian gave the gentleman the nickname of 'Tank top man'. As he passed, he gave us a most unfriendly and slightly intimidating glare. We didn't see this man again on our journeys to school which I was quite relieved about.

Camo Man

On the same day further along our journey to school, we met another man at the 'Zebra' offices. This man was on the opposite side of the bank, at the edge of the building mowing the grass near the river. There are two bridges, which are crossed to get to the offices from the car park. He was well-hidden and couldn't be spotted, except when he moved. The colour of his clothing was dark green, so he blended in really well to the shrubbery around him. He was very busy, so he didn't look up or acknowledge us as we carried on walking through the carpark. It was only when we were crossing one of the bridges that he glanced at us. He was clearly a gardener, but his expression made him seem very threatening and unapproachable; he had a very stern face as well as being very tall and thin. Thankfully we did not meet him again on our walks to school either.

The Bobbers

After the first lockdown in June 2020, we would see two people, a man and a woman, walking together every day. They walked at the same time of day. If we were lucky, we would see them. They were always courteous; they would walk towards us and give us 2 metres apart from them. They would smile at us. Gradually as the Covid restrictions began to ease they would wave and shout hello. This continued right up until Christian left St Pauls School.

"Target Man"

Every morning after lockdown Christian spotted a man in his late 50s, walking towards us. This particular man rarely moved out of the way for us. We could spot him coming as he often wore a Captain America T-shirt (a T-shirt with a target on it). After seeing him a couple of times Christian exclaimed 'He's asking to be shot!". I thought this was an odd thing for Christian to say and when I questioned him on this, he explained that the target symbol on the front of his T-shirt was inviting him to be shot at as he was quite literally, a moving target! It looked like the circles on a clay pigeon board. We soon realised that he walked to the local coffee shop every morning as I used to sometimes spot him on my return journey home. He would walk past the front of our house, heading towards the river, clutching a branded local coffee shop cup!

The 'Walk at You' Postman!

From September 2020 until December 2020, we would meet a postman who would, quite literally, screech his van onto the footpath outside an antique shop on Cores End Road. He would leap out of his van, often not looking before opening his door, to the oncoming traffic. This action caused the cars driving along the main road, to swerve. He was oblivious to this, and he would walk at great speed towards us delivering the post to the terraced houses.

There was always a row of cars parked on the edge of that particular stretch of pavement which already made it narrow to walk along. This postman would storm towards us and elbow us as he past us, without so much as a second thought to our safety or his. Christian called him 'the walk at you postman' and the name stuck. He truly was a man on a mission to deliver his letters, so woe betide anyone who was in his path! This postman was never courteous or polite to us and would smirk as he knocked his way past us. He never once said 'thank you' as we attempted to scuttle out of his path. If we hadn't heard he was behind us, he would weave closely around us – and he never wore a mask! Thankfully we stopped seeing him and since March 2021 the very friendly, happy grey-haired postman is now back on that round.

A Dad, daughter and their dog

Since September 2020 we started to see the 3 of them each morning. They would be crossing the road at

Millside. The Dad would help see his daughter across the very busy and fast-moving road. (Cars drive fast along this stretch, and it is very difficult to gauge their speed). Their black Labrador dog, who is very obedient and off lead, walked to heel next to the Dad. The dog would race across the road when the man gave the command to his dog to cross. The Dad and daughter would always acknowledge us with a smile and a wave. The daughter had very long hair and wore contact lens. She was at St Pauls School with Christian's sister, and she used to wear glasses.

She was always very polite and smiled to Christian, who liked to wave back.

The Headphone Teenager!

From September 2020 we quite often would see a young lad walking towards us, dressed in the local Secondary school uniform. His hair was black, short and curly. He appeared to be quite short, as Christian was much taller than him, and he was petite in build. He always walked at great speed and his walk was jagged and irregular. He wasn't walking in a straight line and seemed to dart about on the pavement. We would often meet this young lad by the clock on Penny's Corner. He looked to be waiting for his friends to arrive on the train. He wore a fashion branded set of headphones (the fashion at the time) on his head. As they are rather large, they made his head look tiny! (Christian knew this lad as he went to St Pauls School with him as well as Scouts).

The 'Businessman'

Christian started to spot a young man in a pale blue suit and called him 'the businessman'. This young man was a teenager and a sixth former! He always looked very smart, wearing a white shirt, black tie and brown pointed leather shoes. A black rucksack was slung over one shoulder. He had long legs and always strode along at speed, rushing to catch a train. He always seemed to walk at us, never once moving out of the way for us. He rarely smiled either. One time this young lad was accompanied by a teenage girl, who Christian thought could be his girlfriend. He referred to it as 'that cringy thing!'

After Covid:

These are a collection of observations made after Covid and all lockdowns:

The 'Grey-shaped' man

Before Lockdown we, very occasionally, saw this gentleman on our walk to school. After lockdown he became a regular person, we would spot every morning. He had black, greasy hair that had grey streaks running through it. The front of his hair was almost white, and the back of his hair grazed his shoulders. He had a greying beard and looked to be in his late fifties. He wore black rimmed glasses and scurried rather than walked. (This gave us the impression he was nervous). Whenever we met this man, he was always by himself. He was not very tall (about Christian's height at the time) and he always wore the same style of clothing too - black T-shirts and dark trousers with white trainers. If it was raining, he would wear a black raincoat. On the odd occasion he wore joggers. This man was always quietly muttering to himself under his breath. We knew he was harmless, so no fear was felt when we saw him. His clothes were often a bit grubby, and his trainers had holes in them. He darted about on the pavement, always careful not to get too close to anyone else.

Another observation Christian made was this gentleman always carried a plastic carrier bag in his hand. He had a habit of looking at the ground and would sometimes stop and pick up something from the ground or out of the bin. It took us a while to work out what he was doing but he was searching for butt ends of cigarettes. He would then place them in his plastic shopping bag. He meant no harm. I always made a point to smile and say hello when we passed him, which worried Christian at the time. I felt sorry for him; Christian was very wary of him. (Now that Christian has left St Paul's School, we often see him walking around the village and I often see him today on a Friday night at a local pub where he enjoys a beer by himself). I quizzed Christian as to why he called this man the 'grey shaped man' and he said, 'because it is always a grey day when we see him'!

The 'Black Man'

We kept seeing a quiet, unassuming fellow feeding the wild blackbirds from his door – He had a stable door that was open on the top half. At first, we would see him standing behind the stable door. He tamed the blackbirds to feed out of his hand during lockdown, especially one. Christian dubbed this blackbird 'the tail-less blackbird' as it had some of its tail feathers missing so it couldn't fly too far. He seemed a nice man. Christian liked him and he felt an instant connection with this man. The gentleman began to smile and wave at us, and Christian would smile and wave back. He lived on a corner in a small, terraced house with a tiny path. Christian simply called him ‘the black man’ because he fed the wild blackbirds.

As time went on the man began to sit on his doorstep calmly watching and feeding the blackbirds. He would hold out his hand and the blackbirds would come and feed from it. That is how tame the blackbirds had become. Christian found this fascinating to watch. At times the blackbirds would circle above the man and then land. Sometimes as they swooped down to land, they would skim the top of Christian's head! Christian was not alarmed in any way. This gentleman would be there most mornings at 8.15am. This became a good incentive to encourage Christian to be ready on time to walk to school every day – and he was. Christian was always eager to take time to watch this man every morning.

The Tennis Guy

During Year 6 when we were walking to school, we would spot a young lad walking past us most mornings on his way to school. It turned out that Christian knew him. He used to be a member of the Tennis club where Christian plays tennis every week. This lad would walk past Christian every morning and neither of them acknowledged each other.

One morning Christian piped up ‘You wouldn’t think we knew each other, would you, Mum? I play tennis with him every Saturday. He’s in the older group mostly but I do occasionally play against him’. I was shocked by this revelation. Christian continued ‘It’s not cool to talk to me, I guess’. This revelation revealed to me how

Christian accepts people not acknowledging him. He was not hurt or upset in any way, whereas most children Christian's age would think this rude and hurtful.

'Bum Hole' Man

On one occasion during our walk to school, Christian noticed a man in a hole at the end of Wharf Lane repairing something underground. He was bent over, and one could not avoid seeing his bottom as we walked past! We caught each other's eye, looked away and giggled. Christian thought the man looked as if he worked for either the telephone exchange or for a local water supplier; he wore a bright fluorescent orange jacket and white helmet. Although we didn't see his face, we definitely think he was a man due to the style of the pants and the trousers he wore. They had slipped down so low that his bare bottom was revealed! Hence the name Christian whispered to me.

The Blonde teenager

Another regular person we saw most mornings was a lad who used to go to school at St Paul's School and who was in Christian's sister's class. He would be walking to the local Secondary school when we would spot him in the mornings. This lad was always friendly, polite and courteous. He would often step aside, either into a person's driveway or between 2 parked cars on the edge of the road to let us pass. We did our best to do the same for him as the path was never wide enough for more than 2 people. He always thanked us every time we moved out of the way for him. Occasionally before Covid, he would be accompanied by another lad from Mollie's class. That lad never moved out of the way unlike the blonde teenager we saw every day.

When Covid hit, we switched pavements due to roadworks that had caused the other pathway to be even narrower. This same lad would wave at us across the street. Since June 2021 the blonde teenager walked by himself. I said to Christian one morning that this blonde teenager was 'a heartbreaker' meaning he is attractive, tall, blonde haired and blue eyed which will draw the attention of the girls.

The 'Bald Jogger'

From March 2021 we started to see this man. We thought he must have taken early retirement, as he looked to be in his early 60s. We would often meet him on Princes Road, heading towards the footpath that led onto Hollands Farm. He always wore the same clothes – a T shirt with blue joggers and white trainers. This jogger would often say 'good morning'. He would be jogging along the edge of the road when we were walking towards him on the narrow footpath, to keep us all safe with 2 metres distance apart, (thus adhering to the social distancing rules). Christian dubbed him the 'bald jogger' simply because the man had lost all of his hair and was jogging.

'The Creepy One!'

We started to see this gentleman every morning in May 2021. This young man (who looked to be in his late 20s), struck Christian as being very odd-looking. He was always neat, tidy and clean; lean and tall. One morning, he came striding towards us which petrified Christian. One could see straight away that he had physical disabilities. He struggled to walk so staggered and lurched whilst moving forwards. This young man shuffled his feet too and his gait was very uneven. He had black hair that was cut to the nape of his neck, and it moulded around the shape of his head. He also had striking facial features such as a very pointed nose and chin. The gentleman spoke loudly to himself as he passed us and his fingers were scrunched up and bent over like talons, which he constantly rubbed together. Occasionally he flapped his hands. (These actions are common amongst people on the autistic spectrum and a clear sign that they are agitated or nervous. By doing these motions he was self-regulating and helping himself to keep calm and less agitated). He appeared nervous. This unnerved Christian who was really scared of him. He decided to call him 'The Creepy One' because he made Christian feel unnerved. This young man often wore a tracksuit or polo neck t-shirt, jumper and dark trousers. He was a very harmless man; just in his own world and going about his day. Christian felt threatened by his presence, but there was nothing to be afraid of as he was a very innocent person.

Sporty Man

Christian started to regularly spot a young man, in his late 20s, follow us out of Bourne End. He always strode past us in a hurry and turned into Furlong Road, often wearing dark sports clothes, armed with a rucksack slung on his back and with his hands in his pockets. This young man was very respectful and always past us with plenty of room between us. He never spoke, but strode around us, nipping in front of us at great speed.

Polite Young Man

Another dark-haired young man would pass us on his way to Bourne End as we were walking towards Wooburn Green. Wearing a dark suit and tie, he too would step off the curb and walk around us. He looked like a sixth former, aged between 16 and 18. If we moved out of the way first, he always politely said a courteous ‘thank you’. We usually saw him at the bottom of New Road. We were very grateful to him for he was always trying to avoid us.

Unloving Dad

On a particularly warm morning whilst walking to school, we witnessed a father and his son on a motorbike together. The son was going to St Paul's School, and he was a pillion, (a passenger riding on the back of the motorbike). Neither were wearing a crash helmet or protective gear! Instead, both were wearing shorts and T-shirts. Whilst witnessing this Christian piped up 'that guy must really hate his kid'. Christian explained to me that, who in their right mind would let a year 5 student on the back of a moped and without a helmet? Christian realised this was a very dangerous and careless thing to do as well as being illegal. I was relieved and pleased that Christian knew how dangerous this act had been.

FUNNY SAYINGS

In this section I have recorded some sayings which show Christian's wit and dry humour. He often says it as it is, which is typical of his neuro divergent brain.

One morning Christian piped up, 'Wet feet again, Mummy, the grass is so wet.' He added, 'wet shoes, wet socks….it's a by-product of walking to school!' The rain that had fallen overnight had not drained away and had made the path extremely wet and treacherous to walk on. We were more careful after that.

A friend asked Christian as we were walking to school, how was he going to get to his new secondary school. Christian answered, 'By the Mum mobile.'

Whilst watching a clip from the film 'Eurovision', Christian blurted out 'She looks like an angry wasp!' He was referring to the scene where there is a sing-athon at a party. The singer in question arrives in a stretch limousine to the party and walks down the red carpet. She is wearing a yellow and black dress.

When we drove past a local Secondary school heading into Marlow, Christian piped up 'this school looks small from the outside but is massive when you get inside there!' He had been around the school and it felt like a Tardis – it is deceivingly bigger inside than it looks from the outside.

As we were talking about making friends Christian said, ‘My body is my friend. I will never be alone. My soul is me. I take my body everywhere with me, so I always have a friend.’ I love this as it gives a clear insight into the way an autistic child views the world.

Driving back from Beaconsfield a huge gust of wind blew through my car as we had the windows fully down, due to it being a really warm day. As we crossed the bridge above the M40, it caused my car to swerve a little. Christian spoke up and said in a loud voice ‘Good grief! I was nearly blown fully out of the car! Mummy slow down!’ I found this really funny as I was only doing 30mph. The gust of wind had taken him by complete surprise and it made us both laugh.

Once a week Christian had a guitar lesson and I was the one who carried it to school for him. One morning I complained about banging my head on the guitar (it had back straps, so the top of the guitar (the headstock) used to sometimes catch the back of my head when I was walking). Christian stopped walking, turned round to me and said, 'You think you've got it bad....my trousers feel as if they might fall down any minute'. Admittedly his trousers were loose around his waist. It was so random that I roared with laughter.

Christian doesn't remember jokes or often get them, but whilst walking to school one morning he said, 'What do you get if you cross Harry Potter with King Arthur?' I couldn't answer so he continued 'The boy who would be king'. It was a very logical and well thought out answer.

A Little Respect

After lockdown when the 2 metre rule of keeping that distance apart from others was enforced, Christian began to notice that not many people adhered to this rule. Very few people would stand aside to let us by. We were the ones ending up on the grass verges to avoid other walkers or runners. Barely anyone said, 'thank you' either. Christian found it quite a shock that this occurred daily. People walking towards us expected us to move aside for them, so when, on the very odd occasion, someone did this for us, Christian would say, in a loud voice, 'That was kind, nobody else moves out of the way for us, Mummy, what a nice person!' Every time he said this I would really chuckle.

Bending Daddy's ear

On one occasion, whilst we were walking to school, Christian asked me when would it be possible for him to own an X Box One? It was something he really wanted and kept talking about. (Part of an autistic trait is that the person can become obsessed about something. At this time Christian was fixated on wanting an X Box One and kept talking about it; Christian's dad was getting irritated by the constant asking). I asked Christian to stop 'bending Daddy's ear'; an old-fashioned expression meaning for Christian to stop talking about it with his Dad. Christian looked very serious at me and retorted 'No I wouldn't do that. His ears would become elf ears and that wouldn't be nice for him!' I really laughed as I knew Christian hadn't understood what I meant.

WILDLIFE SIGHTINGS

I would like to dedicate this section to Mrs Baskerville and the late Paul Carter, who worked at St Paul's School, and who loved keeping an eye on Slate Meadow and its wildlife. (All these sightings occurred when Slate Meadow was a horse field and before building work began):

Birds

Redwings

One morning we saw a very rare sighting of 3 Red Wings together, sitting in one of the weeping willow trees by Slate Meadow. These were the first Red Wings Christian had seen on our walk to school, though we had the seen the same type of bird near our house during lockdown whilst on our bird spotting walks.

Bird in the Chimney

On one occasion, just before we were due to leave for school, Christian was watching TV with his sister. Both looked at each other as they heard a bird tweeting in the chimney but neither of them said anything. I called

Christian to get ready for school and he reluctantly did, leaving the TV on in the lounge as his sister left to go to Secondary school. A couple of minutes passed, and I rushed into the lounge to turn the TV off and as I did, an adult jackdaw flew out of the chimney at precisely the same time! I screamed and ran out of the room! Christian roared with laughter as he thought it was hilarious. We opened the French doors and in due course it flew away. Christian has laughed hysterically over this incident ever since.

The White Egret

Since we started walking to school, we would, quite often, spot a white Egret in the River Wye chalk stream, situated between the grass bank at Brookbank and Slate Meadow. It is so graceful, elegant, beautiful, sleek and much smaller in stature than a heron. We would see the white Egret standing patiently, as still as a statue (exactly like a heron would), on the rocks or on fallen branches in the middle of the stream. The slightest disturbance of a person or dog walking along Brookbank would cause it to fly away.

The White Egret is a very shy and rare sighting in Buckinghamshire, although we know that they are very common in the rivers of Devon and Cornwall where there can be many pairs of them grouped together. (The most we have seen at any one time together is in Looe River where we saw over 23 of them!) They are so majestic and regal and are a joy to spot.

During 2021 we began spotting a pair of them on this stretch of water which is very exciting. Their white feathers are brilliant white like the feathers of a swan. We feel so lucky to have spotted the 2 White Egrets together.

The 'Dive-Bombing Kite'

Every day we used to see Red Kites in Slate Meadow. They would swoop and circle in the sky above the ponies. One morning a Red Kite was swooping down around the horse field as we walked by, but as it swooped, it grazed the top of Christian's head! Being so low we think it was enjoying the air stream under its wings. The wind was very strong and blowing in every direction. It must have lost control a little. Surprisingly, seeing a

Red Kite that close up didn't make Christian frightened. Instead, he looked up and took in the bird's detail. He described the Red Kite as 'magnificent, graceful and large'.

The Jackdaw Jungle

During the month of May 2021, we regularly took the path through the offices at the bottom of Furlong Road. There were so many jackdaws to be found. Whilst taking this path we would have to duck and walk carefully under the low hanging branches that sheltered the path. Due to the number of jackdaws we kept seeing as they pecked the gravel for grubs, Christian nicknamed this area 'the Jackdaw jungle'.

'Daring chimney Jackdaws'

We regularly spotted Jackdaws flying around a particular group of houses and their chimney pots along Cores End Road. When they stopped flying, they tended to strut around the tops of the chimneys, looking down inside them. Christian gave them the name 'daring chimney jackdaws'.

So many robins!

Whenever we walk anywhere, we always spot a robin either hopping along a path close to us or sat in a tree singing its heart out. Christian always spotted a robin on our daily walks to school. On some days we would see several and Christian would count them as we went by. On several occasions however he would see so many that he would lose count of how many he had spotted around us. Christian suggested we called our walk to school 'the many robins walk!'

Kamikaze sparrows

Very often whilst walking along Princes Road (which is set back from Cores End Road in Bourne End), we would spot many fast-flying sparrows leave and descend off one particular roof. The sparrows would fly around us, circling us very closely, but never once hit us. Christian called them the 'Kamikaze sparrows'.

Herons

We often spotted herons along the River Wye chalk stream. Christian liked to observe them so we would often pause and watch them from a distance. Christian liked to see them fly away because he was amazed by the size of their magnificent wingspan. Invariably they did fly away as they realised that we were near them.

Pheasants and partridges

Quite often we would spot several pheasants and partridges running around in Slate Meadow. Christian would spot them and burst out laughing because of the way they would run. He would heartily giggle.

They would puff out their chests, arch their backs, lift their heads high whilst their little legs would be moving so fast, propelling themselves forward, along the field. It really was a very entertaining and humorous sight to behold. Hearing Christian chuckle made me laugh as much as watching this display.

ANIMALS

Ponies

There was a herd of ponies that were kept on Slate Meadow. The ponies were owned by travellers. Christian used to worry sometimes about the welfare of the ponies. The owners would feed them bread and hay, and occasionally, they didn't have any food to eat at all. The ponies would have to scramble into the River Wye chalk stream to drink, which couldn't have been easy for the young foals. The RSPCA used to check on them regularly, but they seemed happy enough about their welfare. The men handled them gruffly and shouted sharply at the ponies on the very rare occasion we did see someone. The owners always checked on them especially when a foal was due.

Everyone was relieved to see the ponies kept on this field. The ponies were a great attraction for young and old alike. (Sadly, at the time of writing, the ponies have been moved off the land and houses are being built where once the ponies roamed. It is a very sad sight to behold. Building work started early 2023).

The barbed wire incident

One morning Christian noticed some loose barbed wire fencing. He was really worried that the ponies would get tangled up in it. When I had dropped Christian off to school, I entered the field and tried to move it but it was impossible without barbed wire cutters. St Paul's School kept a telephone number for the owner, and I was able to contact the gentleman who came out very quickly to fix the problem. Christian was so relieved about this.

The new pony

Quite often new ponies were introduced to the herd of horses that were kept on Slate Meadow. One morning a new beautiful looking piebald hackney pony arrived. Being new to the herd its arrival unsettled the other horses in the field. It took quite a while for the other horses to accept him. The original herd grouped around the new pony, racing and circling it. The new pony seemed very unfazed by the chaotic behaviour of the herd. Due to the temperament of the new pony, they soon accepted him into their herd. For Christian it was fascinating to watch.

Birth of a new foal.

One May morning, whilst walking up Stratford Drive, we noticed a young foal had been born. It was only a few minutes old as its mother was still licking the foal clean. It was an amazing sight. The foal stood up on very shaky legs and reached under its mother's belly for milk. Thankfully it was a warm morning and the sun shone on the new foal. Over the following months we would stop to check on the foal. We saw it grow into a very strong and fast pony.

Escaped Ponies

One morning, having parked and walked from Brookhouse Drive, we discovered two women and two young ponies by Cores End roundabout. A young foal had escaped from the field; it had crossed the river to get to lush grass. The mother of the foal had followed it. The foal was frightened but very hungry. (Brookbank is a very busy stretch of road and the women were trying to herd both the mare and the foal back into the field).

Luckily and very fortuitously, we had a bag of carrots with us to feed to the herd that day, so we handed them to the women who were so grateful. (We often brought a bag of carrots to school so Christian could feed all the ponies). The women were successful in encouraging the ponies back across the stream. Christian was very frightened, which the young foal sensed, so I ushered Christian away to school, leaving the women to handle the ponies. Thankfully a police car pulled up as we were heading to school.

By the time I had returned, after dropping Christian to school, peace was restored once more. There was no sign of the police, or the two women and the ponies were safely back in their field where they belonged. (There was no fencing to keep the ponies in the field, so the same problem did occur several times). The ponies needed access to the stream for water as there was no water trough in the field. Also, when there was no grass to eat in the field, the temptation was too great for the ponies. They would wade across the stream to the lush grass on the other side of the stream to eat! Thankfully, soon after this incident, the owners repaired the fence, allowing the ponies access to the stream, and fed the ponies more regularly. The escapes were very infrequent after that.

Dead Foal in a Field

This was a very upsetting, alarming and sad sight to see. A very new foal hadn't made it through the night. It had been left, and the other ponies were huddled together away from it. One could see blood, so I quickly ushered Christian into school, alerting Paul the caretaker about it. We were told the owner had been called and would be doing something quickly to remove it. By the time Christian's school day was over, the foal had been removed from the field. Christian felt great sadness for the mother of the foal for a good few days after this incident.

Two Muntjacs

On one particular morning we had the most unexpected encounter. We met a muntjac on the bridge at Millboard

Road, who froze and stared at us. It was in the middle of the path! It didn't know which way to run. Thankfully there was a hole in the hedge and the muntjac went through it. Christian was convinced it would dash out onto the busy A4155 road and collide with a car, but thankfully it didn't and the muntjac was safe once more. This muntjac was very beautiful to look at. Christian remembered his shiny black nose and brown eyes most of all. It was very handsome, looked young and lean.

A few days later the same incident happened again. Christian was convinced, (and I was relieved to think), that it was the same muntjac.

We spotted quite a few muntjacs over the years of walking to school. They were, mostly on Slate Meadow. On the odd occasion we have seen a pair of them together in the horse field which is very special. The Muntjacs seemed to like being with the ponies in this field, grazing happily in the sunshine. Maybe it's safety in numbers. The ponies didn't seem to mind sharing their field with them. Muntjacs are very wary of us humans, yet they are such a joy to see.

A Dead Badger

One time, when Christian was very young, we found a dead badger lying on the pavement. We had to walk past it. The Badger was very long and large. Having never seen a badger before, Christian was very curious. He noticed it had a lot of white teeth, and two very long incisor teeth. Its black nose was shaped just like a dog's nose, and it was so straight and pointed. The badger had surprisingly small ears. (They are rare to see in this area, so it was very sad to think it had been run over by a passing vehicle). By the time Christian came home from school that day, it had been removed. For a long time afterwards Christian wondered where it had ended up and who had taken it.

The Worms

Often after a rainstorm we would spot worms on the concrete footpaths as we walked to school. On one occasion Christian counted seeing over 70 during our walk to school! They would cause Christian to scream and do a funny jig which would make me laugh. The pavement from Brook House Drive to St Paul's

School was the worst path for them. The worms appeared in a variety of sizes - long and chubby. Some were long, chubby, others thin or short. No matter what the size of the worm, Christian would scream at it!

OTHER MOMENTS

The Umbrella Moment!

Soon after the first lockdown, we were walking to school on a stormy day that looked like rain was coming. Unusually the road was clear of cars and we were able to cross the Parade without going to the Pelican Crossing. When we reached the pavement, on the other side, I was too busy telling Christian that if anyone came near us then I would use my umbrella like a weapon and point my umbrella at them.

As I was saying this, I was not watching where I was walking, and as I demonstrated what I would do if someone came too close, I said 'on guard!' Whilst thrusting the umbrella forward in front of me. As I did this, I tripped up the pavement and could not save my fall. I went right over and landed face down on the pavement, grazing my knee and my face as I went crashing down!

I was rather badly shaken, and Christian couldn't help but laugh at me. He couldn't control his laughter as he found it so funny! A really nice gentleman came running across the road to help me up, but I couldn't let him do that as Covid was so prevalent. He was so concerned for me that I tried to stand up by myself and carry on as if nothing had happened. However, I didn't get very far as the pain was immense and I started to cry. Christian was still laughing – that is until he saw my tears. He then realised I had in fact badly hurt myself.

As luck would have it, my cousin Gary was filling his van up with petrol at the local petrol Garage along The Parade and came rushing towards me, when he realised it was me and that I was in trouble. Thankfully, he phoned Kev who came to my rescue. We drove Christian to school together that morning due to the amount of pain I was in. (I am relieved to say that I was not seriously injured but I was badly bruised. I had hurt my pride and dignity too!) Looking back, I can smile about what happened. Christian still laughs when we recall this memory together.

The 'Yellow Car' Game

This was a game created by Christian's eldest sister, and it is a game we still play as a family now (usually only on long car journeys). The one who spots a yellow car first gently taps or nudges the person next to them and says, ‘yellow car!’ At first this was a great game; however soon the nudges became punches or thumps thus causing a great distraction to the person driving the car. So, the game was banned from being played inside the car. However, Christian started to search for a yellow car on his walks to school. If he spotted one driving past, or parked, he would pat me and shout ‘yellow car!’ I didn’t mind this version so much because I was not driving and therefore not distracted by it. (We still play this game today, but without the patting element!)

Three Weeping Willow Trees

Just by Slate meadow, along Brookbank path, there were 3 Weeping Willow Trees. Christian's middle sister and Christian gave the 3 trees nicknames - Mummy, Daddy, and Mollie. Christian's sister was a tree hugger and on the odd occasion, when Christian was younger, he would join in with the daily ritual of hugging a tree. Sometimes Christian's sister would place a greeting card at the foot of the tree trunk, especially at Christmas. However, this was not something Christian did. He thought it was a lovely gesture, although a little strange! When Christian's sister moved on to Secondary school Christian stopped hugging the trees. Instead, he liked to swing from the weeping willow trees because of their long, draping and cascading branches. These branches would dangle to the floor. Occasionally Christian would pull on these branches with his whole body weight but they never broke.

Christian enjoyed walking through the trailing branches as they looked like curtains. Sadly, now the Weeping Willow Tree branches are trimmed and kept to a certain height preventing any branches from trailing to the floor. (At the time of writing both the 'Mummy' and 'Daddy' trees have both been cut down. It looks very empty without them).

The Electronic Device Talks

In order to keep Christian engaged whilst walking with me to school, I would encourage him to talk about anything that was on his mind. Invariably this would be Minecraft, Krunker and the need to have a mobile phone! By allowing Christian to chat away, he in turn did not notice the distance of the walk to school. I would nod or say, 'Oh, that's nice' or 'is that so?' when he paused for breath. It helped pass the time on the walk for sure.

The Dreaded Roadworks

Throughout April and May 2021 there were many roadworks relating to cabling being laid underground which linked up from Slough through to Oxford. Consequently, this resulted in the pavement along Cores End Road being dug up to lay them. There were traffic lights on the road but also much of the pavement was closed, making it difficult to navigate one's way safely around them! Fortunately, we have been lucky. One trick we quickly worked out was the timing of when to walk to school in order to avoid a crush on the pavement. Students from the local Secondary school would throng together in large groups of up to ten at a time, which was very daunting during the pandemic. Christian thought they looked like a black swarm. Very few social distancing rules were being adhered to. We were very aware that a lot of secondary school children disembarked their buses at roughly the same time every school morning. We have raced along the pavement to avoid them.

During the road works this was a lot worse. We had to walk on the road when youngsters appeared around a bend at the bottom of Furlong Road. This was very stressful at times. Thankfully our school times changed in 2021 and we didn't have this collision anymore. We learnt very quickly that staying on the right-hand path all the way to Cores End Road was the safest option as most people liked to walk on the left hand footpath.

Falling Trees

On our walks to school, Christian noticed the eradication of several trees including the one outside Bourne for Desserts, one in the car park of St. Dunstan's Church and one on the local green corner at the end of the village. He was quite concerned about this. The two trees outside a local supermarket suddenly disappeared overnight too. It was a great shame when this tragedy occurred. The locals were very upset as these trees were planted to commemorate the late Queen's 25th reign as Queen. This supermarket replaced the trees and two very young ones were planted in their place. Christian hoped the trees would grow quickly in order to provide shelter for the wild birds.

AUTHOR'S NOTES

I would like to thank the real-life people mentioned in this memoir. I loved this time of day with Christian. We started to notice the same people every morning on our journey to school. Slowly, over time, Christian gave these people nicknames. Christian describes the way he sees people and objects in the world. Being on the autistic spectrum his observations are direct and very different from that of a neuro-typical person. It made our walks to school that bit more fun and meaningful. Having autism a routine is essential and greatly needed, so it also encouraged Christian to leave for school at the same time in the mornings, in the hope we would meet the same people on our walk each day.

As I wrote this I found it compelling as it too gives an insight into the ADHD mind and mindset. I used to rush home to jot down Christian's words and descriptions. Sometimes I would type them rapidly into my mobile phone the minute Christian went into school, for fear of forgetting the words he used to describe what he saw. I love the way Christian sees the world; innocent yet poignant.

Christian has had fun helping me put this memoir together as much as I have loved spending the school run hours accompanying him. The writings are solely observations from a child and were recorded with no malice, unkindness, harm or hurt intended.

I hope these memoirs inspire you and make you smile a little, thus making your day that bit lighter, happier and brighter by bringing you some laughter to your day as they have done to mine.

Surprisingly, I thought I would miss our walk to Primary school because it had become so colourful and joyous. However, we still have a drive and a shorter walk to school to Christian's Secondary school and we have already started to make a collection of memoirs of our journeys there!

What will we notice on our journey to Secondary School? It will be interesting for sure. If you have enjoyed this collection of memories, then please look out for our next memoir...

Special thanks to all the staff at The Britannia Pub in Marlow for their kindness whilst I wrote this. (I regularly sat in their beer garden and sometimes inside the pub, with a drink whilst writing and waiting for Christian to come out of school). There have been some extremely warm days whilst compiling this memoir, and having air conditioned area to sit in and write, was extremely helpful and welcome.

Grateful thanks to a fellow author, Anne Main, who has encouraged, supported, inspired and believed in me to publish this memoir. She gave me hope in my darkest days of 2023 as well as giving her time so readily in getting this worked published.

Thanks too, must go to Christian for being such a larger-than-life person – for just being you; for sharing openly and expressing all that you thought and saw during our journeys to school. I have loved every moment and enjoyed recording them to form this memoir for you.

I would like to add my special thanks to my friend Bridget who helped type up my notes before I worked out what to do with them! It was time consuming yet she never complained. I am indebted to you for giving up your time so willingly.

Finally, sincere thanks go to my husband who has encouraged me to write this memoir; for his patience, support and belief in me. He is my rock and my soul mate. May this memoir become a best seller to help us continue to live and provide for our family, making all of our dreams a reality.

Printed in Great Britain
by Amazon

41895840R00086